The Christmas Birthday Story

by Margaret Laurence
Pictures by Helen Lucas

Alfred A. Knopf *New York*

for Daniel—M.L.

and

for Cori—H.L.

This is a Borzoi Book published by Alfred A. Knopf, Inc. Published in the United States by Alfred A. Knopf, Inc., New York. Distributed by Random House, Inc., New York. Manufactured in the United States of America 10 9 8 7 6 5 4 3 2 1

This story is about a newborn baby and his mother and father.
And it's about a great golden star shining in the sky at night.
And it's about three wise kings.
It is called The Christmas Birthday Story.

In the very olden days, in a far-off country, there lived a hard-working carpenter named Joseph. His wife's name was Mary. Joseph and Mary were happy because soon they were going to have a baby. They didn't mind at all whether it turned out to be a boy or a girl. Either kind would be fine with them. They just hoped their baby would be strong and healthy.

One day Joseph told Mary they must go on a trip to a faraway city called Bethlehem, to pay their taxes. Mary was a little worried about going on a trip because it was nearly time for her baby to be born.

"What if we can't find a good place to stay in that city?" she said to Joseph. "Suppose our baby is born there?"

"Don't worry," Joseph said. "Everything will be all right, you'll see."

So off they went. It was the olden days, remember, so they didn't have cars or trains or buses or planes. Mary rode on a donkey, a tame gray donkey with long pointy ears, and Joseph walked beside her.

The little donkey went slowly, so the journey took quite a while. It seemed a long, long way.

When darkness came, Mary and Joseph lay down to rest in the quiet countryside, with only the trees and the sleeping birds around them. The donkey rested, too. When morning came, they went on.

On and on and on they went. *Clip-clop-clip-clop* went the donkey's hooves on the dusty road. Mary and Joseph got very tired. The little donkey got tired, too.

At last they reached the city of Bethlehem. When Mary and Joseph got there, it was night time. They walked through the dark and quiet streets. They looked for a place to stay. But everywhere they asked, they heard the same answer.

"I'm sorry. We have no rooms left. All full. You'll have to go somewhere else."

Joseph felt sad when he could not find a place for them to spend the night.

"I'm sorry you had to come with me," he said to Mary. "It would have been better for you to stay at home after all. Now what shall we do?"

But Mary was a loving person, and she did not want her husband to feel sad.

"Never mind," she said. "You didn't know this city of Bethlehem would be so crowded. Look...there's another place. Shall we try there?"

So they went into that hotel, and it was the last one in the whole city. But the hotel man only shook his head.

"We're all full here, too," he said. "No room anywhere."

Then the hotel man saw how worried Joseph looked, and he saw how tired Mary looked, and he felt sorry for them.

"Wait a minute," he said. "I have an idea. There's a stable outside. You can stay there if you like."

Well, of course Mary and Joseph were really pleased to find somewhere to stay, even if it was only a stable and not a proper house. At least they would be able to rest there. So out they went.

When Mary and Joseph went into that stable, they saw it was a warm and clean place, big and warm and clean. They saw a brown cow standing quietly in her stall. The cow mooed softly. They heard a small lamb saying *ba-a-a* in its small voice, and the mother sheep replied *ba-a-a* in her deeper voice, just as though she were saying to her baby lamb, "Everything is all right...you can go back to sleep now."

Soft yellow hay was piled in the stable. It was the animals' food. The hay had a faint sweet smell. Mary liked the sweet smell of the hay. She went over to the big box where the hay was kept. That hay box was called a manger.

"See, Joseph, this clean sweet hay," Mary said. "I shall make a bed for our baby here, because I think our child will be born this very night."

Lo and behold...that is just what happened. Mary's baby was born that same night. The baby turned out to be a boy, and he was a fine healthy baby, too. When he was born, his mother wrapped him in a small warm blanket and she put him down to sleep in the bed she had made in the manger. The newborn baby slept there on the bed of soft sweet hay while his mother and his father watched him. The cow and the sheep and the lamb and all the other animals kept very quiet, just as though they knew a baby was sleeping there.

On that same evening, three kings were riding across the country. They didn't have horses. They rode on camels. Camels are interesting beasts. They have humps on their backs. They have long necks, too, and they have long, long legs. They can run fast as the wind on their long legs. These camels had shiny leather saddles, and leather reins around their necks. The saddles and reins had tiny silver bells tied on. When the three kings rode their camels, the silver bells went *ting-ring-ting*. The three kings were dressed in green and blue and purple, and they looked very fine.

As they were riding across the country that night, one of the kings suddenly pointed to the sky.

"Look!" he said to the other kings. "Do you see that star shining in the sky over there? I never in my life saw such a bright star."

The other kings looked, and they saw the star, too. It was a great golden star, shining and shimmering in the night sky.

The three kings gazed at it silently. They all felt that the bright starlight was beckoning them on.

"Surely that star will lead us to some wonderful sight," the second king said at last.

The great star seemed to shine even brighter.

"Now I think I can see a city over there," the third king said. "Let's ride over that way."

So off they rode across the country, and the silver bells on their camel saddles went *ting-ring-ting*. At last they reached the city of Bethlehem. Then they noticed a strange thing. The great golden star seemed to be shining and shimmering right above a stable. The three kings felt there must be something special about that place. So they rode over there.

They got down from their camels and opened the stable door. And what did they see?

Mary and Joseph and the baby.

"Good evening," said the tallest king, who wore a golden crown. "May we come in?"

"It's a chilly night, you see," said the middle-sized king, who wore a silver crown, "and we would like to warm ourselves in this warm stable."

"We are also quite tired," said the shortest king, who wore a small silver and gold crown, "and we would like to rest."

Joseph and Mary smiled at the three kings.

"You are welcome," said Joseph. "Please come in. I am Joseph, a carpenter, and this is my wife, Mary. Here, asleep, is our new son—he was just born this very night."

Now when the three kings saw the newborn baby, they all felt that he was special and wonderful. They thought they would like to give presents to him. They looked in the big deep pockets of their green and blue and purple robes, and each one found something to give the baby. The tall king and the middle-sized king both gave bottles of perfume, called frankincense and myrrh, so that Mary could put a little bit of it in the water when she bathed the baby. And the shortest king gave a beautiful carved wooden box all full of gold coins, so that Mary and Joseph would have some money to buy things for their baby.

"Thank you for these gifts," Mary said.

The kings wanted to know the baby's name.

"We are going to call him Jesus," Mary told them. "Do you think that is a good name?"

"Yes," said the three kings. "That is a very good name indeed."

"You are clever men," said Mary, "and you know many things. Tell me what you think this baby will be when he grows up to be a man."

The three kings looked at the baby, and they smiled.

"I think he will be strong and hard-working, like Joseph," the first king said.

"And I think he will be gentle and kind, like his mother," the second king said.

The third king thought for quite a while before he said anything. "I think," he said at last, "that he will be a wise teacher and a friend to all people."

And that is exactly what happened. That child Jesus grew up to be a man, and he was strong and hard-working, like Joseph the carpenter. He was gentle and kind, like Mary his mother. And he was something else, too. He was a wise teacher and a friend to all people.

So we remember him always, and at Christmas time we celebrate his birthday, for Christmas is the very time Jesus was born, long long ago, in the far-off city of Bethlehem.

Margaret Laurence

is the author of highly-praised novels, short stories, and essays for adults, several charming children's books, and has twice been awarded Canada's highest literary honor, the Governor General's Award for fiction. She lives in Lakefield, Ontario.

Helen Lucas

is an award-winning artist whose work has been published, widely exhibited, and is represented in private and public collections in North America and Europe. She lives in Toronto.

Library of Congress Cataloging in Publication Data. Laurence, Margaret. The Christmas birthday story. Summary: The author's interpretation of Jesus' birth and the subsequent visit of the three kings. 1. Jesus Christ—Nativity—Juvenile fiction. [1. Jesus Christ—Nativity—Fiction. 2. Christmas stories] I. Lucas, Helen. II. Title. PZ7.L372784ch 1980 [E] 79-27159 ISBN 0-394-84361-4 ISBN 0-394-94361-9 lib. bdg.